Through
the Gate
of Good

JAMES ALLEN TITLES

Through
the Gate
of Good

James Allen

MEDIA

Published 2019 by Gildan Media LLC
aka G&D Media
www.GandDmedia.com

Design by Meghan Day Healey of Story Horse, LLC

Library of Congress Cataloging-in-Publication Data is available upon request

ISBN: 978-1-7225-0246-1

10   9   8   7   6   5   4   3   2   1

Contents

Foreword

The series of articles which comprise this book appeared in serial form in the third volume of "The Light of Reason," and it is in compliance with the earnest request of readers and the importunities of friends that I now reprint them in book form.

The articles are reprinted as they were originally published, with the addition of the Introduction.

—James Allen

Introduction

The genius of the present age in matters spiritual is toward simplicity, and the hunger of the human heart is for Truth, naked and uninvolved. That hunger will eventually bring about (is already bringing about) its own satisfaction, and here and there are men and women who, passing through the gateway of self-conquest, are entering into possession of the transcendent righteousness.

The closing years of the nineteenth century witnessed the culmination of formalism, and the spiritual reaction is now firmly established. Already

the end
Of old faiths and beginning of the new

is discernible to all who have removed from their mental vision somewhat of the textual dust of dying creeds, and have penetrated, however faintly, that sublime region of Truth which is discoverable only by practice, and which is made manifest by pure thoughts and holy deeds.

The universal decay of effete religious systems which the world is witnessing today is matter for rejoicing; it is the death which precedes life; it is the passing away of the false in order that the true may be more fully revealed. The true can, at worst, but remain hidden. It endures. It remains forever. Its invincibility cannot be qualified, and he who has had but one momentary glimpse of the true can never again be anxious for its safety. That about which men are anxious is the false, which they mistake for the true, and this, in spite of all their anxiety, must fade away at last.

In the lives of all the great teachers we see a manifestation of that universal truth, the majesty and splendor of which is as yet but dimly comprehended by mankind, but which must, during the gradual transformation and transmutation which the accumulating ages shall effect, at last become the possession of all. That Truth, as manifested by the teachers, was written by them, as it only can be written, in thoughts and deeds of the loftiest moral excellence which have been permanently impressed upon the mind of mankind by their embodiment in preceptial form. It is to the sweet lives and inspiring words of these mighty teachers that the eyes of a hungering and thirsting world are again being turned, and the light of life is being lighted up, the world over, in hearts that are ready to attune themselves to the eternal song of love and peace. What religions have failed to do, religion will accomplish: what the priest has obscured, the Spirit of truth in the heart of man will make plain, and the world is now finding spiritual healing and refreshment in turning away from traditional and historic accretions, and going back to the pure fountain of Truth as revealed so simply, clearly, and beautifully by blameless teachers, and which has its inexhaustible spring within themselves.

To aid men and women (more particularly those in Christian countries) to find this abiding Truth more speedily, these articles, setting forth the life and precepts of Jesus, were written. Formalism and self are heavy burdens to carry, and in directing the minds of men to blamelessness of conduct and purity of heart, I know I can leave the result with the supreme law, and that there are those who will read and, having read, will pass from the burdensome complexities of ignorance and formalism to the joyful simplicity of enlightenment and Truth.

—James Allen

The Gate
and the Way

Strait is the gate, and narrow is the way, which
leadeth unto life: and few there be that find it.

—Jesus

A good man out of the good treasure of the
heart bringeth forth good things.

—Jesus

The supreme aim of all religions is to teach men
how to live; and the learning and the living are
religion itself. The purification of the human
heart, the building up of a blameless life, and the
perfecting of the soul, these are the great underly-
ing and enduring factors in all religions and creeds
the world over. That which is vital in every religion
is the striving after and the practice of goodness; all
things else are accretions, superfluities, illusions.

Goodness—and by goodness I mean sinlessness—is the beautiful and imperishable form of religion, but creeds and religions are the perishable garments, woven of the threads of opinion, in which men clothe it. One after another religions come and go, but Religion, being Life itself, endures forever. Let men cease to quarrel over the garments and strive to perceive the universality and beauty of the indwelling form; thus will they become wedded to it, will become one with the supreme goodness. Religion is goodness; goodness is religion.

We know nothing higher than goodness. We can conceive of nothing more beautiful than goodness. Beholding the perfect goodness, men call it God. Seeing that goodness practiced by man, men worship him as God.

We behold Jesus as a sinless man; in him is the perfect goodness revealed, not obscurely and metaphysically, but in all his words and deeds; and it is by virtue of his sinlessness that he is accepted as an exemplar and universal teacher.

The teachers of mankind are few. A thousand years may pass by without the advent of such a one; but when the true teacher does appear, the distinguishing feature by which he is known is his life. His conduct is different from that of other men, and his teaching is never derived from any man or book, but from his own life. The teacher first lives, and then teaches others how they may likewise live. The proof and witness of his teaching is in himself, his life. Out of millions of preachers, one only is ultimately accepted by mankind as the true teacher, and the one who is thus accepted and exalted is *he who lives*. All the others are mere disquisitionaries and commentators, and as such they rapidly pass out of human ken.

Jesus, the teacher, lived, in all its perfection and in the face of the most adverse conditions, the divine life of love; he pursued the true life of good will, as distinguished from the false life of self-seeking, which the majority elect to follow. In him there was no element of selfishness, all his thoughts, words, and acts being prompted by the Spirit of love. To this Spirit of love he so entirely subjected his personality that he became one with it, so much so that he literally became divine love personified. His complete victory over the personality was accomplished by obedience to the divine law of love within himself, by virtue of which he became divine; and his whole teaching is to the effect that all who will practice the same obedience will realize the same divine life, will become consciously divine.

The unalterable meekness, undying compassion, sweet forgiveness, and unending love and patience of Jesus are the themes of a thousand hymns, the subjects of millions of heartfelt prayers; and this is so because those qualities are recognized everywhere and by all men as being distinctively divine. To make the practice of these qualities the chief object of life constitutes religion; to deny them, and to continue to live in their selfish opposites—pride, condemnation, harshness, hatred, and anger— constitutes irreligion.

Men everywhere, in their inmost hearts, though they may deny it argumentatively, know that goodness is divine; and Jesus is worshiped as God, not for any claim he made, nor because of any miraculous circumstance connected with his life, but because he never departed from the perfect goodness, the faultless love. "God is love, love is God." Man knows no God except love manifesting in the human heart and life in the form of stainless thoughts, blameless words, and deeds of gentle pity and forgiveness; and he can only know this God in the measure that he has realized love in his own heart by self-subjugation. The God which forms the subject of theological argument, and whose existence or nonexistence men are so eager to prove, is the God of hypothesis and speculation. He who, by overcoming self, has found, dwelling within him, the supreme love, knows that that love is far beyond the reach of all selfish argument and can *only be lived*; and he lives, leaving vain argument to those who wilt not come up higher.

Having, by obedience, entered into full possession of the divine life, Jesus gave to the world certain spiritual rules, by the observance of which all men could become sons of God, could live the perfect life. These rules or precepts are so simple, direct, and unmistakable that it is impossible to misunderstand them. So plain and unequivocal are they that even an unlettered child could grasp their meaning without difficulty. All of them are directly related to human conduct, and can be applied only by the individual in his own life. To carry out the spirit of these rules in one's daily conduct constitutes the whole duty of life, and lifts the individual into the full consciousness of his divine origin and nature, of his oneness with God, the Supreme Good. It is here, however, where the difficulty arises, for, although there are millions of men and women worshiping Jesus as God in a miraculous or metaphysical sense, there are really very few who believe in his precepts, and who attempt to carry them out in their lives. In the precepts themselves there can be no difficulty or misunderstanding; all this lies in the unbelief of those who read the precepts. Men do not carry out the precepts of Jesus because they do not believe it possible to do so, and so they never try; whilst there are others who, though believing it possible and necessary to carry them out, are not willing to make the personal sacrifices which those precepts demand. Yet, apart from the earnest striving to live out the teachings of Jesus there can be no true life. Merely to call Jesus "Lord" does not constitute discipleship, but to weave his words into the fabric of one's life, to put into execution his divine and self-perfecting precepts, this, and this only, constitutes discipleship.

Let it be understood thus early that with the almost innumerable creeds which have been built upon the Hebrew scriptures, I have absolutely nothing to do. I have to do entirely with the life and teaching of Jesus, and with the vital realities in the human heart to which that teaching is directed. I have to do with goodness, not with speculation; with love, not with theological theories; with self-perfection, not with fleeting opinions.

Jesus was a supremely good man; this all men know, and to know this is all-embracing and all-sufficient. He has left precepts which, if a man will guide his conduct by them, will lead him unerringly to the supreme goodness; to know this is gladdening and glorious.

A good man is the flower of humanity, and to daily grow purer, nobler, more Godlike, by overcoming some selfish tendency, is to be drawing continually nearer to the divine heart. "He that would be my disciple let him deny himself daily," is a statement which none can misunderstand or misapply, howsoever he may ignore it. Nowhere in the universe is there any substitute for goodness, and until a man has this he has nothing worthy or enduring. To the possession of goodness there is only one way, and that is *to give up all and everything that is opposed to goodness.* Every selfish desire must be eradicated; every impure thought must be yielded up; every clinging to opinion must be sacrificed; and it is the doing of this that constitutes the following of Christ. That which is above all creeds, beliefs, and opinions is a loving and self-sacrificing heart. The life of Jesus is a demonstration of this truth, and all his teaching is designed to bring about this holy and supreme consummation.

To dwell in love always and toward all is to live the true life, is to have life itself. Jesus so lived, and all men may so live if they will humbly and faithfully carry out his precepts. So long as they refuse to do this, clinging to their desires, passions, and opinions, they cannot be ranked as his disciples—they are the disciples of self. "Verily, verily, I say unto you: whosoever committeth sin is the servant of sin," is the searching declaration of Jesus. Let men cease to delude themselves with the belief that they can retain their bad tempers, their lusts, their harsh words and judgments, their personal hatreds, their petty contentions, and daring opinions, and yet have Christ. All that divides man from man, and man from goodness is not of Christ, for Christ is love. To continue to commit sin is to be a doer of sin, a follower of self, and not a doer of righteousness and a follower of Christ. Sin and Christ cannot dwell together, and he who accepts the Christ life of pure goodness ceases from sin. To follow Christ means to give up all, in our mind and conduct, that antagonizes the spirit of love; and this, we shall find as we proceed, necessitates complete self-surrender, refusing to harbor any thought that is not pure, compassionate, and gentle. The Christ Spirit of love puts an end, not only to all sin, but to all division, and contention. If I contend for an opinion, say, about the divinity of Jesus Christ, against the opinion of another as to his nondivinity, I at once create division and strife, and depart from the Christ, the spirit of love. When Christ is disputed about, Christ is lost. It is no less selfish and sinful to cling to opinion than to cling to impure desire. Knowing this, the good man gives up himself unreservedly to the Spirit of love, and dwells in love toward all, contending with none, condemning none, hating none, but loving all, seeing behind their opinions, their creeds, and their sins, into their striving, suffering, and sorrowing hearts. "He that loveth his life shall lose it." Eternal life belongs to him who will obediently relinquish his petty, narrowing, sin-loving, strife-producing personal self, for only by so doing can he enter into the large, beautiful, free, and glorious life of abounding love. Herein is the path of life; for the strait gate is the gate of goodness, and the narrow way is the way of renunciation, or self-sacrifice. So strait is the gate that no sin can pass through, and so narrow is the way that he who essays to walk it can take with him no selfish thought as his companion.

The Law
and the Prophets

Therefore all things whatsoever ye would that
men should do to you, do ye even so to them:
for this is the law and the prophets.

–Jesus

If thou wilt enter into life, keep the
commandments.

–Jesus

The commandments and precepts of Jesus were
given to men to be kept. This is so simple and
self-evident a truth that there ought to be no
necessity to state it; yet, after the precepts of Jesus
have been before the world for nearly nineteen
hundred years, this necessity not only exists, but
is very great, so widespread is the belief that the
tasks embodied in the precepts are not only utterly

impracticable, but altogether impossible of human accomplishment. This disbelief in the possibility of carrying out the divine commands is the primary delusion, due to ignorance, in which men are caught, and it is impossible for any man to comprehend spiritual things until he destroys it.

The words of Jesus are the direct outcome of an intimate knowledge of divine law, and his every utterance is in harmonious relationship with the eternal substance. This a man finds as he molds the spiritual life contained in those words into his own life—that is, as he succeeds in living the precepts.

Let us now examine these precepts and see how they are to be carried out and what they imply and involve. Most of them are embodied in the Sermon on the Mount, and all of them are directly related to individual conduct, so that there are only two possible ways of dealing with them, namely, to practice them, or to ignore them.

It is not necessary for me to refer to them all separately, as not only have my readers the Bible at their command, but each precept is based upon the same divine principle, and to learn the spirit of one is to know the spirit of them all. Indeed, seeing that not only all the precepts, but that the whole duty of life in its human and divine relationship has been embodied in the seventeen words, "all things whatsoever ye would that men should do to you, do ye even so to them," it is only necessary to refer to the other precepts in order to elucidate the carrying out of this one, for in learning this one precept, the whole range of spiritual life and knowledge is involved: "This is the law and the prophets."

The precept is extremely simple; this is why men have failed to understand it and to put it into effect. Its application, however, to the soul of the individual leaves no room for selfishness and self-compromise, and so comprehensive is it that to carry it out in its entirety means the attainment of Christlike perfection of character. But before a man can put it into practice, *he must strive to understand it,* and even this initial step necessitates a self-surrender which few are willing to make. A man can learn nothing unless he regards himself as a learner. Before a man can learn anything of the divine spirit within, he must come to the feet of Christ divested of all his desires, his opinions and views, yea, even of his cherished ideal, regarding himself as a little child, knowing nothing, blind and ignorant, seeking knowledge. Before this attitude of humility is adopted, the attainment of divine life and knowledge is impossible; but he who will adopt it will rapidly enter into the highest revelations, and the carrying out of the precept will soon become easy and natural to him.

Having clothed himself with humility the first questions a man asks himself are: "How am I acting toward others?" "What am I doing to others?" "How am I thinking of others?" "Are my thoughts of and acts toward others prompted by unselfish love, as I would theirs should be to me, or are they the outcome of personal dislike, of petty revenge, or of narrow bigotry and condemnation?" As a man, in the sacred silence of his soul, asks himself these searching questions, applying all his thoughts and acts to the spirit of the primary precept of Jesus, his understanding will become illuminated so that he will unerringly see where he has hitherto failed; and he will also see what he has to do in rectifying his heart and conduct, and the way in which it is to be done. Such a man has become a disciple of Christ at whose feet he sits, and whose commands he is prepared to carry out no matter at what sacrifice to himself.

One hour's daily meditation upon this precept, combined with a sincere wish to learn its meaning and a determination to carry it out, would rapidly lift a man above his sinful nature into the clear light and freedom of divine Truth, for it would compel him to remodel his entire life and to turn right round in his attitude toward others. Let a man, before acting, ask himself the question, "Should I like others to do this to me?" and he will soon find his way out of his spiritual darkness, for he will then begin to live for others instead of for himself; will adjust his thoughts and conduct to the principle of divine love, instead of blindly following his selfish inclinations. However others act toward him, he will begin to act toward all in a calm, quiet, forgiving spirit. If others attack his attitude, his beliefs, his religion, he will not retaliate; and will cease from attacking others, realizing that it is his supreme duty to carry out his divine Master's commands; and the carrying out of those commands will demand the readjustment, not only of his thoughts and acts, but of every detail of his life, even down to his eating and drinking and clothing. As he proceeds in this new life, the teachings of Jesus will become luminous with a new light, vital with a new life, and he will feel that every precept is for him and that he must carry them out, ceasing to accuse others because they do not carry them out. As he reads the words, "Judge not," he will know that he must cease from all harsh and unkind judgment, that he must think kindly of all, just as much so of those who are unkind to him as of those who are kind to him; that if others judge and condemn him, he must not do so to them, and, putting aside all personal considerations, must deal with them in the spirit of equity, wisdom, and love. It will thus be seen that even in carrying out the one simple precept, "Judge not," a man must necessarily rise above much that is merely personal and selfish, and will develop unusual spiritual strength. This course of conduct, diligently pursued, will lead to the observance of the precept, "Resist not evil," for if a man ceases to judge others as evil, he will cease to resist them as evil. Of late years much has been written about nonresistance to evil, but he who would comprehend the spiritual significance of this, or indeed of any precept, must not rest content with mere dialectic definitions of it, but must assiduously *practice it*; he can only find its meaning by *doing it*. And in the doing of this precept, a man will destroy in himself the eye of evil, and in its place he will learn to look through the eye of good, the eye of Truth, when he will see that evil is not worth resisting and that the practice of the good is supremely excellent.

Whilst a man is engaged in resisting evil, he is not only not practicing the good, he is actually involved in the like passion and prejudice which he condemns in another, and as a direct result of his attitude of mind, he himself is resisted by others as evil. Resist a man, a party, a law, a religion, a government as evil, and you yourself will be resisted as evil. He who considers it as a great evil that he should be persecuted and condemned, let him cease to persecute and condemn. Let him turn away from all that he has hitherto regarded as evil, and begin to look for the good, taking passion, resentment, and retaliation out of his heart, and he will very soon see that what he has all along been resisting as evil has no existence as such, and that it was merely an exaggerated and illusionary reflection of the passion and the folly which were in himself. So deep and far-reaching is this precept that the practice of it will take a man far up the heights of spiritual knowledge and attainment; and when, by following its demands, he has so far purified and over come himself as to see good and not evil in all men and all things, he will then be prepared to carry out a still higher precept (though one contained in the primary precept), namely, "*Love your enemies.*"

Over none of the precepts do men stumble more than this one, and the cause for such stumbling is near at hand and very plain. It is to be expected that men who regard fighting, retaliation, and hatred toward their enemies as indications of nobility of character should look upon this precept as not only an impracticable but a very foolish command. And from their standpoint of knowledge they are right. If man be regarded as a mere animal cut off from the Divine, those fierce, destructive qualities which are esteemed noble in the beast are noble in man.

To such men, living in their animal qualities and instincts, meekness, forgiveness, and self-denying love appear as cowardice, effeminacy, and weak sentimentality. If, however, we recognize in man certain divine qualities (more active in some than in others, but possessed in a measure by all), such as love, purity, compassion, reason, wisdom, and so forth, which lift him above the animal, then the precept, "Love your enemies," not only appears practicable but is seen to represent the rightful and legitimate state of man. To the man, therefore, who says, "This is an impossible precept," I would say: "You are right; to you it is impossible; but only your unbelief in the efficacy of those qualities which constitute goodness, and your belief in the power of the animal forces, make it so; reverse your attitude of mind, and the impossibility will fade away."

No man can carry out and understand this precept who is not willing to renounce his animal nature. He who would find the Christ (the pure Spirit of truth) must cease to warp and blind his spiritual vision by flattering his feelings and passions. The source of all enmity within himself must be destroyed. Hatred is none the less hatred when it is called dislike. Personal antipathies, however natural they may be to the animal man, can have no place in the divine life. Nor can a man

see spiritual things or receive spiritual truth while
his mind is involved in malice, dislike, animosity,
revenge, or that blind egotism which thinks "I (in
my views) am right, and you are wrong." The keep-
ing, then, of the commandment, "Love your enemies," necessitates the removal from the heart of
all hatred and egotism, and as this is accomplished,
the principle of divine love, which is unchangeably
the same toward all—the just and the unjust, the
sinful and the saintly—takes the place, in the consciousness, of those violent animal and personal
loves which are continually changing, and coming
and going, and which are inseparably linked with
their opposite of violent hatred. It is impossible to
love one's enemies whilst living in the animal personality, for that personality is of the very nature
of blind love and hatred; it is only by deserting the
personal elements that the impersonal, divine love,
which does not alter with the changing attitudes of
others, is found and can become the dominating
factor in one's conduct; and when that is done, the
disciple realizes that his true nature is divine.

The love, then, that enables a man to deal
kindly with his enemies and to do to others as he
would like others to do to him, irrespective of *their*
attitudes of mind, is not an emotion, impulse, or
preference, but a state of divine knowledge arrived
at by practice; and as this knowledge is perfected

in the mind, the eternal principles of the divine law of which the prophets spoke, and on which they stood, are comprehended.

He who will keep the precepts of Jesus will conquer himself and will become divinely illuminated. He who will not keep them will remain in the darkness of his lower nature, shut out from all understanding of spiritual principles and of the divine law. Herein, also, resides the infallible test of discipleship, for it was none other than Jesus the Christ who said, "He that loveth me not keepeth not my sayings," and "He that hath my commandments, and keepeth them, he it is that loveth me."

The Yoke and the Burden

Take my yoke upon you, and learn of me; for
   I am meek and lowly in heart; and ye shall
   find rest unto your souls.
For my yoke is easy, and my burden is light.

                                                —Jesus

Be ye therefore perfect, even as your Father
   which is in heaven is perfect.

                                                —Jesus

Humanity is essentially divine. Every precept of
Jesus rests upon this truth. If man were not
divine, the precepts would be both worthless and meaningless, as there would be nothing
within him (no divine spirit) to which they could
appeal. The very fact that man is capable of loving his enemies and of returning good for evil is

an attestation of his inward and essential divinity. If sin were man's natural and rightful condition, it would be right that he should remain in it and there would be no necessity to exhort him to virtue and holiness, for it would be impossible for him to act otherwise than in accordance with his original nature. Whenever men exhort their fellows to virtue, nobility of action, purity of thought, and unselfishness, they unconsciously assert and emphasize man's originally divine nature, and proclaim, though perhaps they know it not, his superiority to sin and his Godlike power to overcome it.

So long, however, has man dwelt in the habitations of sin that he has at last come to regard himself as native to it and as being cut off from the divine source, which he believes to be outside and away from him. He has thereby lost the consciousness and knowledge of his own divinity, of his essential oneness with God, the spirit of good. Humanity at present is in the position of the prodigal son, wandering in the far country of sin and attempting to live upon the swinish husks of base desires and false beliefs; and every divine precept and command is a call to man to return to his Father's house, his original innocence, and to recover and reëstablish the knowledge of his substantial oneness with the Divine.

The whole of the teaching of Jesus is an exhortation to men to do as he did, to live as he lived; he thereby recognizes and affirms the inherent equality of humanity with himself, and in declaring, "I and my Father are one," he speaks not alone for himself but for all men. The difference between the life of Jesus and that of other men is not arbitrarily imposed, nor does it exist in essentiality; it is self-imposed and exists in individual choice. Jesus fully recognized his oneness with the Father (the divine source), and lived consciously in that oneness; other men (speaking broadly) not only do not recognize their oneness with the Divine, but do not believe it; it is therefore impossible for them, by virtue of their unbelief, to rise to the dignity and majesty of the divine life. Whilst a man regards himself as being the creature of sin, believing himself to be originally degraded, he must necessarily remain degraded, and subject to sin; but let him *realize* that he is originally divine, that he is not, never was, and never can be cut off from the Divine except in his own ignorance and willful choice, and he will at once rise above sin and begin to manifest the divine life.

Man is primarily a spiritual being, and as such is of the nature and substance of the eternal Spirit, the unchangeable reality, which men call God. Goodness, not sin, is his rightful condition; perfection, not imperfection, is his heritage, and this a man may enter into and realize *now* if he will grant the condition, which is the denial or abandonment of self, that is, of his feverish desires, his proud will, his egotism and self-seeking—all that which St. Paul calls the "natural man."

In the Sermon on the Mount, Jesus describes the way of action and thought by which the divine life is to be lived, and after having laid down the whole duty of man as a spiritual being, a son of God, he exhorts men to live as becomes their divine relationship, in the words, "Be ye therefore perfect, even as your Father which is in heaven is perfect." In sounding this high call to perfection, Jesus, far from commanding an impossibility, merely urges men to live their true life of divine perfection and to give up their false life of self-seeking and sin.

The "yoke" which Jesus calls upon men to take upon themselves is the yoke of obedience— obedience to the divine nature which is in every man, no longer obeying the lower desires and impulses; and the "burden" is the burden of a sinless life. Such a yoke is "easy," because it entails no suffering; and such a burden is "light," for it is relieved of the weight of sorrow, anxiety, and fear. It is the life of self-seeking which is so uneasy, while the burden of sin, even of the mildest forms of sin, is heavy and wearisome. To know the truth of this, a man has only to look around upon the world, and then within his own soul.

Jesus recognized the divine in all men, even those called "evil," and he dwelt upon it and reiterated it. The idea of man's being *innately* degraded, a lost creature, incapable of lifting himself to the heights of goodness and righteousness, nowhere enters into either the words, conceptions, or teaching of Jesus. On the other hand, the whole of his teaching affirms and emphasizes man's innate goodness and his unlimited capacity for practicing goodness. When he says, "Condemn not and ye shall not be condemned; forgive and ye shall be forgiven; give and it shall be given unto you; good measure pressed down, shaken together, and running over shall *men* give into your bosoms," he plainly tells us that if we will put away all resentment and treat others with kindness, forgiveness, and gentle consideration, we shall then find that men are so intrinsically good that they will heap kindnesses without number upon us. He who would find how good at heart men are, let him throw away all his ideas and suspicions about the "evil" in others, and find and practice the good within himself.

Jesus also speaks of the "righteous," of those who "hunger and thirst for righteousness," of "the meek," "the merciful," "the pure in heart," and "the peacemakers," and declares that all such are blessed. He draws our attention to the fact that those who regard themselves as evil are so far from being evil that they know how to give good gifts to their children, and that even the publicans and sinners return love for love. His testimony to the guileless innocence of little children seems to have been much overlooked and ignored by those who call themselves his followers; and in all his references to and treatment of the fallen, he looks behind and away from the surface defilement (other men regard this as the real man, and dwell upon and exaggerate its enormity), and sees and brings forth the divine beauty and goodness hidden away under the accumulation of sin.

He spoke of sinners as "captives" and "blind," and stated that it was his mission to preach deliverance and restore sight, clearly indicating that sin is foreign to man and that sinlessness is his true state; and he even declared that men shall do greater works than He did.

Nowhere in the whole range of history or inspiration is there to be found such testimony to the lofty nobility and essential purity and goodness (doubtless more or less latent) of the human heart as is found in the words and deeds of Jesus. In his divine goodness he knew the human heart, and he knew that it was good.

Man has within him the divine power by which he can rise to the highest heights of spiritual achievement; by which he can shake off sin and shame and sorrow, and do the will of the Father, the supreme good; by which he can conquer all the powers of darkness within, and stand radiant and free; by which he can subdue the world, and scale the lofty pinnacles of Truth. This can man, by choice, by resolve, and by his divine strength, accomplish; but he can accomplish it only in and by obedience; he must choose meekness and low-liness of heart, he must abandon strife for peace, passion for purity, hatred for love, self-seeking for self-sacrifice, and must overcome evil with good; for this is the holy Way of Truth; this is the safe and abiding salvation; this is the yoke and burden of the Christ.

The Word and the Doer

Whosoever heareth these sayings of mine, and doeth them, I will liken him unto a wise man which built his house upon a rock: and the rain descended, and the floods came, and the wind blew, and beat upon that house; and it fell not: for it was founded upon a rock.

–Jesus

If ye continue in my word, then ye are my disciples indeed; and ye shall know the truth, and the truth shall make you free.

–Jesus

The Gospel of Jesus is a Gospel of *living and doing*. If it were not this, it would not voice the eternal truth. Its temple is purified conduct, the entrance door to which is self-surrender. It invites men to shake off sin, and promises, as a result, joy and blessedness and perfect peace.

There is one characteristic in the teachings of all those great souls who have been worshiped by mankind as saviors, and that is that they bring to light, and appeal directly to, the simple facts and truths of the soul and of life; and in the teaching of Jesus this feature stands out preeminently. Strictly speaking, he put forward no theory, advanced no creed, laid no claim to any particular "views," and propounded no speculative philosophy. He was content to state that which is.

Men are so taken up with their pleasures, theories, theologies, and philosophies that they cannot apprehend the simple facts of life, and it is supremely the office of the true teacher to bring men back to the simple and beautiful realities of their own souls. The false teacher, he who cannot perceive the simple truths of duty and of conduct, and does not see himself and other men as they are, when asked to point out the way of Truth will declare that it lies entirely in the acceptance of his own particular theology, and will warn the questioner against all other systems of theology. Not so, however, the true teacher, he who knows the human heart, and who sees life as it is; and particularly not so, Jesus, who, when questioned of the way of life, always told his questioner to go and do certain things. Never once did he refer a questioner to any views, theories, or deftly woven philosophies of his own, or indeed of other men. He referred them to duty and to purity of life and conduct, and the only things he warned them against were their own sins. And, truly, this is all that is needful. A man either abandons sin or he clings to it; if the former, he does all and realizes the law of life; if the latter, he does nothing, and remains ignorant, blind, without understanding. Truth is contained in conduct, and not in any system of thought; and to live purely and blamelessly is Infinitely superior to all wordy doctrines. Let a man carefully study every system of theology, and he will at last find that one selfless thought, one pure deed, puts them all to shame. Truth is divorced from the controversies of the creeds, but it shines with undimmed luster in the self-forgetting deed. How beautifully this is illustrated in the parables of Jesus, and how forcibly is it brought out in many of the incidents of his life; particularly in that one recorded in the 10th chapter of Luke, where the lawyer asks, "Master, what shall I do to inherit eternal life?" The answer of Jesus is to ask him to repeat the chief commandment, which being done, Jesus simply says, "This do, and thou shall live." Whereupon, the lawyer, wishing to draw Jesus into an argument in order, no doubt, to confound him, asks, "And who is my

neighbor?" We then have the incomparable parable of the Good Samaritan, wherein Jesus shows
in the simplest language and imagery, yet forcibly
and unmistakably, that religious observances are
so many vain and useless burdens unless accompa-
nied by good deeds, and that the so-called worldly
man who does unselfish deeds has already found
eternal life; while the so-called religious man who
shuts up his soul against mercy and unselfishness
is shut out from life. To comprehend the full force
of this parable it is necessary to bear in mind that
the priests and the Levites were regarded by the
Jews as being the highly favored and chosen of
God, whereas the Samaritans were regarded as
being entirely outside the pale of salvation.

Jesus recognized no religion outside conduct;
and truly there is none. Pure goodness is religion,
and outside it there is no religion. There are innumerable doctrines, and there is much strife and
heated controversy, but a man is only truly religious when he succeeds in rising above these and
this, and reaches that loving place in his heart
where all hateful distinctions are burned away by
the pure flames of compassion and love. And in
this divine place Jesus stood, and he calls other
men thither to receive rest and peace. That Jesus
was meek and lowly and loving and compassionate
and pure is very beautiful, but it is not sufficient; it

is necessary, reader, that you also should be meek and lowly and loving and compassionate and pure. That Jesus subordinated his own will to the will of the Father, it is inspiring to know, but it is not sufficient; it is necessary that you, too, should likewise subordinate your will to that of the overruling Good. The grace and beauty and goodness that were in Jesus can be of no value to you, cannot be understood by you, unless they are also *in you*; and they can never be in you until you *practice* them; for, apart from *doing*, the qualities which constitute goodness do not, as far as you are concerned, exist. To adore Jesus for his divine qualities is a long step toward Truth, but to practice those qualities is Truth itself; and he who truly adores the perfection of another will not rest content in his own imperfection, but will fashion his soul after the likeness of that other. To us and to all there is no sufficiency, no blessedness, no peace to be derived from the goodness of another, not even the goodness of God; not until the goodness is *done* by us, not until it is, by constant effort, incorporated into our being, can we know and possess its blessedness and peace. Therefore, thou who adorest Jesus for his divine qualities, practice those qualities thyself, and thou too shalt be divine.

The teaching of Jesus brings men back to the simple truth that righteousness, or right-doing, is

entirely a matter of individual conduct, and not a
mystical something apart from a man's thoughts
and actions, and that each must be righteous for
himself; each must be a doer of the word; and it
is a man's own doing that brings him peace and
gladness of heart, not the doing of another.

Millions of people worship Jesus and call him
Lord, but Jesus does not leave us in any difficulty
or doubt as to who are his disciples, as to who have
entered into life; his words are simplicity itself:
"Not every one that saith unto me, Lord, Lord,
shall enter into the kingdom of heaven; but he that
doeth the will of my Father which is in Heaven;"
and again, "Why call ye me Lord, Lord, and do not
the things which I say?" And they are the doers of
the Father's will who shape their conduct to the
divine precepts.

The doer of the word demonstrates and proves
its truth in his own mind and life. He thus knows
the eternal rock as a substantial reality within
himself, and he builds thereon the temple of righteousness which no rains of grief, no winds of
temptation, and no floods of sin can destroy or
undermine. It is only the *doer* of forgiveness who
tastes the sweets of forgiveness; it is only he who
practices love and mercy and righteousness who
receives into his heart the overflowing measure
of their blessedness; and none but he who dwells

in peace toward all can know the boundless and immeasurable peace. Thus is the doer of the word the disciple indeed, and continuing in that word, becoming one with it in heart and mind, he knows the Truth which frees the soul from the bondage of sin.

The Vine and the Branches

I am the vine, ye are the branches. He that
abideth in me, and I in him, the same
bringeth forth much fruit: for without
me ye can do nothing.

—Jesus as the Christ

Come unto me, all ye that labour and are
heavy laden, and I will give you rest.

—Jesus as the Christ

The Christ is the spirit of love, which is the abiding and indwelling reality in man. Yet though its perfected temple is the human form, and it can only visibly and consciously manifest itself in and through the human personality, it is impersonal in its nature, is a universal and eternal principle, and is at once the source and the substance of life.

In this principle of love, all knowledge, intelligence, and wisdom are contained, and until a man realizes it as the one vital reality of his being, he does not fully comprehend the Christ. Such glorious realization is the crown of evolution, the supreme aim of existence. Its attainment is complete salvation, emancipation from all error, ignorance, and sin.

This principle is in all men, but is not manifested by all; and it is not known and manifested by men because they continue to cling to those personal elements which obscure its presence and power. Every personal element in human nature is changeable and perishable, and to cling to them is to embrace negations, shadows, death. In the material world, an object cannot be perceived until all intervening obstacles are removed; and in the spiritual region an abiding principle cannot be apprehended until every impermanent element is relinquished. Before a man can know love as the abiding reality within him, he must utterly abandon all those human tendencies which frustrate its perfect manifestation. By so doing he becomes one with love—becomes love itself; he then discovers that he is, and always has been, divine and one with God.

Jesus, by his complete victory over the personality, realized and manifested his oneness with the supreme spirit; and, subordinating his entire nature and life to impersonal love, he became, literally, an embodiment of the Christ. He is therefore truly called the Christ.

When Jesus said, "Without Me ye can do nothing," he spoke not of his perishable form, but of the universal spirit of love of which his conduct was a perfect manifestation; and this utterance of his is the statement of a simple truth; for the works of man are vain and worthless when they are done for personal ends, and he himself remains a perishable being, immersed in darkness and fearing death, so long as he lives in his personal gratifications. The animal in man can never respond to and know the divine; only the divine can respond to the divine. The spirit of hatred in man can never vibrate in unison with the spirit of love; love only can apprehend love and become linked with it. Man is divine; man is of the substance of love; this he may realize if he will relinquish the impure, personal elements which he has hitherto been blindly following, and will fly to the impersonal realities of the Christ Spirit; and these realities are purity, humility, compassion, wisdom, love.

Every precept of Jesus demands the unconditional sacrifice of some selfish, personal element

before it can be carried out. Man cannot know the
real whilst he clings to the unreal; he cannot do
the work of Truth whilst he clings to error. Whilst
a man cherishes lust, hatred, pride, vanity, self-
indulgence, covetousness, he can do nothing, for
the works of all these sinful elements are unreal
and perishable. Only when he takes refuge in the
Spirit of love within, and becomes patient, gentle,
pure, pitiful, and forgiving, does he work the works
of righteousness and bear the fruits of life. The
vine is not a vine without its branches, and even
then it is not complete until those branches bear
fruit. Love is not complete until it is *lived* by man;
until it is fully understood by him and manifested
in his conduct. A man can only consciously ally
himself to the vine of love by deserting all strife
and hatred and condemnation and impurity and
pride and self-seeking, and by thinking only loving
thoughts and doing loving deeds. By so doing, he
awakens within him the divine nature which he
has heretofore been crucifying and denying. Every
time a man gives way to anger, impatience, greed,
pride, vanity, or any form of personal selfishness,
he denies the Christ, he shuts himself out from
love. And thus only does one deny Christ, and not
by refusing to adopt a formulated creed. Christ is
known only to him who by constant striving has
converted himself from a sinful to a pure being,

who by noble, moral effort has succeeded in relinquishing that perishable self which is the source of all suffering and sorrow and unrest, and has become rational, gentle, peaceful, loving, and pure.

Man's only refuge from sin is sinless love, flying to and dwelling in which, and abandoning all else as evanescent, unreal, and worthless, daily practicing love toward all in heart and mind and deed, harboring no injurious or impure thoughts—he discovers the imperishable principles of his being, enters fully into the knowledge of his oneness with eternal life, and receives the never-ending rest.

Salvation
This Day

This day is salvation come to this house.

        –Jesus to Zacchæus

Behold, the kingdom of God is within you.

           –Jesus

I have tried to show, in the five foregoing chapters, that the teaching of Jesus is based entirely on the perfection of conduct, and can be summed up in the one word "goodness." Jesus manifested this goodness in his life, and his teaching is vitally powerful because it is rooted in his life, his conduct. His command, "Follow me," is literal and actual, not in the sense of a slavish imitation of the external details of his life, but in scaling (as he scaled) the heights of goodness and pity and love by the conquest of self. The glory of his teaching is embodied in his precepts, as the splendor of his life is wrapped up in them; and he who adopts those precepts as the guides of his life will so perfect his conduct by purifying the inward springs of thought and action as to become a spiritualized and sin-less being, fulfilling the whole duty of life and the purpose of existence. Herein also is contained complete salvation, namely, freedom from sin.

The word "salvation" is mentioned by Jesus only twice, and only one of these utterances (that to Zacchæus) can be said to have any vital significance for us; yet in that one brief statement we are fully enlightened as to its meaning by virtue of its pointed application to the altered conduct of Zacchæus. This man, we infer, had hitherto been hard, exacting, and grasping, but though he had not yet seen in person the new teacher, his message had reached his ears, and he had opened his heart to the good news that man can and should repent, and abandon selfish and sinful practices for good and sinless conduct. And this he had done, and, having proved its blessedness, no wonder that when Jesus came to his house he "received him joyfully," and told him how he had abandoned wrong-doing for right-doing; evil for good; the self-ish for the unselfish life. Jesus did not inquire into the "religious views" of Zacchæus; did not impose upon him any change of view or opinion; did not demand that he believe anything about Jesus as being the Messiah, the Son of God, and so forth. Zacchæus had *changed his conduct*; had completely turned round in his attitude toward others; had abandoned greed for generosity, extortion for charity, honesty for dishonesty, selfishness for unselfishness, evil for good—and this was sufficient, as Jesus declared in the words, "This day is salvation come to this house."

The only salvation recognized and taught by Jesus is salvation from sin, and the effects of sin, *here and now*; and this must be effected by utterly abandoning sin, which, being done, the kingdom of God is realized in the heart as a state of perfect knowledge, perfect blessedness, perfect peace.

"Except a man be born again, he cannot see the kingdom of God." A man must become a "new creature," and how can he become new except by utterly abandoning the old? That man's last state is worse than his first who imagines that, though still continuing to cling to his old temper, his old opinionativeness, his old vanity, his old selfishness, he is constituted a "new creature" in some mysterious and unexplainable way by the adoption of some particular theology or religious formula. A man can be said to be born again, to be a new creature, to be saved from sin, only when he turns round on his old, natural, selfish self, and denies

and abandons it. Only by putting away forever the
old temper, the old opinionativeness, the old vanity, the old selfishness, the old life of self in any or
every shape, only by doing this and turning to the
new life of gentleness and purity and humility and
unselfish love can a man be said to be saved from
sin; and then he is saved indeed, for, no more practicing it, it can trouble him no more. Herein also is
heaven, not a speculative heaven beyond the tomb,
but a real, abiding, and ever-present heaven in the
heart; a heaven from which all the hellish desires
and moods and sufferings are banished, where
love rules, and from which peace is never absent.

Good news indeed is that message of Jesus
which reveals to man his divine possibilities;
which says in substance to sin-stricken humanity,
"Take up thy bed and walk;" which tells man that
he need no longer remain the creature of darkness and ignorance and sin if he will but believe in
goodness, and will watch and strive and conquer
until he has actualized in his life the goodness that
is sinless. And in thus believing and overcoming,
man not only has the guide of that perfect rule
which Jesus has embodied in his precepts, he has
also the inward guide, the Spirit of truth in his
own heart, "the light which lighteth every man
that cometh into the world," which, as he follows

it, will infallibly witness to the divine origin of those precepts.

He who will humbly pass through the gate of good, resolving that every element of his nature that is not pure and true and lovable shall be abandoned, that every violation of the divine precepts shall be abolished, to him, faithful, humble, true, will be revealed the sublime vision of the perfect one, and, day by day purifying his heart and perfecting his conduct in accordance with his vision, he will sooner or later rise above all the subtleties of his lower nature, will wash away every ignominious stain from his soul, and realize the perfect goodness of the eternal Christ.

James Allen: A Memoir

By Lily L. Allen

from *The Epoch* (February–March 1912)

> *Unto pure devotion*
> *Devote thyself: with perfect meditation*
> *Comes perfect act, and the right-hearted rise—*
> *More certainly because they seek no gain—*
> *Forth from the bands of body, step by step.*
> *To highest seats of bliss.*

James Allen was born in Leicester, England, on November 28th, 1864. His father, at one time a very prosperous manufacturer, was especially fond of "Jim," and before great financial failures overtook him, he would often look at the delicate, refined boy, poring over his books, and would say, "My boy, I'll make a scholar of you."

The Father was a high type of man intellectually, and a great reader, so could appreciate the evident thirst for education and knowledge which he observed in his quiet studious boy.

As a young child he was very delicate and nervous, often suffering untold agony during his school days through the misunderstanding harshness of some of his school teachers, and others with whom he was forced to associate, though he retained always the tenderest memories of others—one or two of his teachers in particular, who no doubt are still living.

He loved to get alone with his books, and many a time he has drawn a vivid picture for me, of the hours he spent with his precious books in his favourite corner by the home fire; his father, whom he dearly loved, in his arm chair opposite also deeply engrossed in his favourite authors. On such evenings he would question his father on some of the profound thoughts that surged through his soul— thoughts he could scarcely form into words—and the father, unable to answer, would gaze at him long over his spectacles, and at last say: "My boy, my boy, you have lived before"—and when the boy eagerly but reverently would suggest an answer to his own question, the father would grow silent and thoughtful, as though he *sensed* the future man and his mission, as he looked at the boy and listened to his words—and many a time he was heard to remark, "Such knowledge comes not in one short life."

There were times when the boy startled those about him into a deep concern for his health, and they would beg him not to *think so much*, and in after years he often smiled when he recalled how his father would say—"Jim, we will have you in the Churchyard soon, if you think so much."

Not that he was by any means unlike other boys where games were concerned. He could play leap-frog and marbles with the best of them, and those who knew him as a man—those who were privileged to meet him at "Bryngoleu"—will remember how he could enter into a game with all his heart. Badminton he delighted in during the summer evenings, or whenever he felt he could.

About three years after our marriage, when our little Nora was about eighteen months old, and he about thirty-three, I realized a great change coming over him, and knew that he was renouncing everything that most men hold dear that he might find Truth, and lead the weary sin-stricken world to Peace. He at that time commenced the practice of rising early in the morning, at times long before daylight, that he might go out on the hills—like One of old—to commune with God, and meditate on Divine things. I do not claim to have understood him fully in those days. The light in which he lived and moved was far too white for my earth-bound eyes to see, and a *sense of it only* was beginning to dawn upon me. But I knew I dare not stay him or hold him back, though at times my woman's heart cried out to do so, waiting him all my own, and not then understanding his divine mission.

Then came his first book, "From Poverty to Power." This book is considered by many his best book. It has passed into many editions, and tens of thousands have been sold all over the world, both authorized and pirated editions, for perhaps no author's works have been more pirated than those of James Allen.

As a private secretary he worked from 9 a.m. to 6 p.m., and used every moment out of office writing his books. Soon after the publication of "From Poverty to Power" came "All These Things Added," and then "As a Man Thinketh," a book perhaps better known and more widely read than any other from his pen.

About this time, too, the "Light of Reason" was founded and he gave up all his time to the work of editing the Magazine, at the same time carrying on a voluminous correspondence with searchers after Truth all over the world. And ever as the years went by he kept straight on, and never once looked back or swerved from the path of holiness. Oh, it was a blessed thing indeed to be the chosen one to walk by the side of his earthly body, and to watch the glory dawning upon him!

He took a keen interest in many scientific subjects, and always eagerly read the latest discovery in astronomy, and he delighted in geology and botany. Among his favourite books I find Shakespeare, Milton, Emerson, Browning, The Bhagavad-Gita, the Tao-Tea-King of Lao-Tze, the Light of Asia, the Gospel of Buddha, Walt Whitman, Dr. Bucke's Cosmic Consciousness, and the Holy Bible.

He might have written on a wide range of subjects had he chosen to do so, and was often asked for articles on many questions outside his particular work, but he refused to comply, consecrating his whole thought and effort to preach the Gospel of Peace.

When physical suffering overtook him he never once complained, but grandly and patiently bore his pain, hiding it from those around him, and only we who knew and loved him so well, and his kind, tender Doctor, knew how greatly he suffered. And yet he stayed not; still he rose before the dawn to meditate, and commune with God; still he sat at his desk and wrote those words of Light and Life which will ring down through the ages, calling men and women from their sins and sorrows to peace and rest.

Always strong in his complete manhood, though small of stature physically, and as gentle as he was strong, no one ever heard an angry word from those kind lips. Those who served him adored him; those who had business dealings with him trusted and honoured him. Ah! how much my heart prompts me to write of his self-sacrificing life, his tender words, his gentle deeds, his knowledge and his wisdom. But why? Surely there is no need, for do not his books speak in words written by his own hand, and will they not speak to generations yet to come?

About Christmas time I saw the change coming, and understood it not—blind! blind! blind! I could not think it possible that *he* should be taken and *I* left.

But we three—as if we knew—clung closer to each other, and loved one another with a greater love—if that were possible—than ever before. Look at his portrait given with the January "Epoch," and reproduced again in this, and you will see that even then our Beloved, our Teacher and Guide, was letting go his hold on the physical. He was leaving us then, and we didn't know it. Often I had urged him to stop work awhile and rest, but he always gave me the same answer, "My darling, when I stop I must go, don't try to stay my hand."

And so he worked on, until that day, Friday, January 12, 1912, when, about one o'clock he sat down in his chair, and looking at me with a great compassion and yearning in those blessed eyes, he cried out, as he stretched out his arms to me, *"Oh, I have finished, I have finished, I can go no further, I have done."*

Need I say that everything that human aid and human skill could do was done to keep him still with us. Of those last few days I dare scarcely write. How could my pen describe them? And when we knew the end was near, with his dear hands upon my head in blessing, he gave his work and his beloved people into my hands, charging me to bless and help them, until I received the call to give up my stewardship!

"I will help you," he said, "and if I can I shall come to you and be with you often."

Words, blessed words of love and comfort, *for my heart alone* often came from his lips, and a sweet smile ever came over the pale calm face when our little Nora came to kiss him and speak loving words to him, while always the gentle voice breathed the tender words to her—*"My little darling!"*

So calmly, peacefully, quietly, he passed from us at the dawn on Wednesday, January 24, 1912. "Passed from us," did I say? Nay, only the outer garment has passed from our mortal vision. He lives! and when the great grief that tears our hearts at the separation is calmed and stilled, I think that we shall know that he is still with us. We shall again rejoice in his companionship and presence.

When his voice was growing faint and low, I heard him whispering, and leaning down to catch the words I heard—"At last, at last—at home—my wanderings are over"—and then, I heard no more, for my heart was breaking within me, and I felt, for *him* indeed it was *"Home at last!"* but for me—And then, as though he knew my thoughts, he turned and again holding out his hands to me, he said: "I have only one thing more to say to you, my beloved, and that is I love you, and I will be waiting for you; good-bye."

I write this memoir for those who love him, for those who will read it with tender loving hearts, and tearful eyes; for those who will not look critically at the way in which I have tried to tell out of my lonely heart this short story of his life and passing away—for *his* pupils, and, therefore, my friends.

We clothed the mortal remains in *pure white linen*, symbol of his fair, pure life, and so, clasping the photo of the one he loved best upon his bosom—they committed all that remained to the funeral pyre.

About the Author

James Allen was one of the pioneering figures of the self-help movement and modern inspirational thought. A philosophical writer and poet, he is best known for his book *As a Man Thinketh*. Writing about complex subjects such as faith, destiny, love, patience, and religion, he had the unique ability to explain them in a way that is simple and easy to comprehend. He often wrote about cause and effect, as well as overcoming sadness, sorrow and grief.

Allen was born in 1864 in Leicester, England into a working-class family. His father travelled alone to America to find work, but was murdered within days of arriving. With the family now facing economic disaster, Allen, at age 15, was forced to leave school and find work to support them.

During stints as a private secretary and stationer, he found that he could showcase his spiritual and social interests in journalism by writing for the magazine *The Herald of the Golden Age.*

In 1901, when he was 37, Allen published his first book, *From Poverty to Power.* In 1902 he began to publish his own spiritual magazine, *The Light of Reason* (which would be retitled *The Epoch* after his death). Each issue contained announcements, an editorial written by Allen on a different subject each month, and many articles, poems, and quotes written by popular authors of the day and even local, unheard of authors.

His third and most famous book *As a Man Thinketh* was published in 1903. The book's minor popularity enabled him to quit his secretarial work and pursue his writing and editing career full time. He wrote 19 books in all, publishing at least one per year while continuing to publish his magazine, until his death. Allen wrote when he had a message—one that he had lived out in his own life and knew that it was good.

In 1905, Allen organized his magazine subscribers into groups (called "The Brotherhood") that would meet regularly and reported on their meetings each month in the magazine. Allen and his wife, Lily Louisa Oram, whom he had married in 1895, would often travel to these group meetings to give speeches and read articles. Some of Allen's favorite writings, and those he quoted often, include the works of Shakespeare, Milton, Emerson, the Bible, Buddha, Whitman, Trine, and Lao-Tze.

Allen died in 1912 at the age of 47. Following his death, Lily, with the help of their daughter, Nora took over the editing of *The Light of Reason*, now under the name *The Epoch*. Lily continued to publish the magazine until her failing eyesight prevented her from doing so. Lily's life was devoted to spreading the works of her husband until her death at age 84.